Screws

by Anne Welsbacher

Consultant:
Philip W. Hammer, Ph.D.
Assistant Manager of Education
American Institute of Physics

Bridgestone Books
an imprint of Capstone Press
Mankato, Minnesota

Bridgestone Books are published by Capstone Press
151 Good Counsel Drive, P.O. Box 669, Mankato, Minnesota 56002
http://www.capstone-press.com

Library of Congress Cataloging-in-Publication Data
Welsbacher, Anne, 1955–
     Screws/by Anne Welsbacher.
     p. cm.—(The Bridgestone Science Library)
     Includes bibliographical references and index.
     Summary: Uses everyday examples to show how screws are simple machines that
make joining things together, moving, and lifting easier.
     ISBN 0-7368-0613-X
     1. Screws—Juvenile literature. [1. Screws.] I. Title. II. Series.
TJ1338.W45 2001
621.8'82—dc21
                                                                                    00-025614

Editorial Credits
Rebecca Glaser, editor; Linda Clavel, cover designer; Kia Bielke, illustrator; Katy Kudela,
     photo researcher

Photo Credits
David F. Clobes, cover, 8, 18
Jack Glisson, 12, 14
Kate Boykin, 4, 10
Kimberly Danger, 16 (inset)
Root Resources/Phyllis Cerny, 20
Unicorn Stock Photos/Richard Baker, 16

1 2 3 4 5 6 06 05 04 03 02 01

Table of Contents

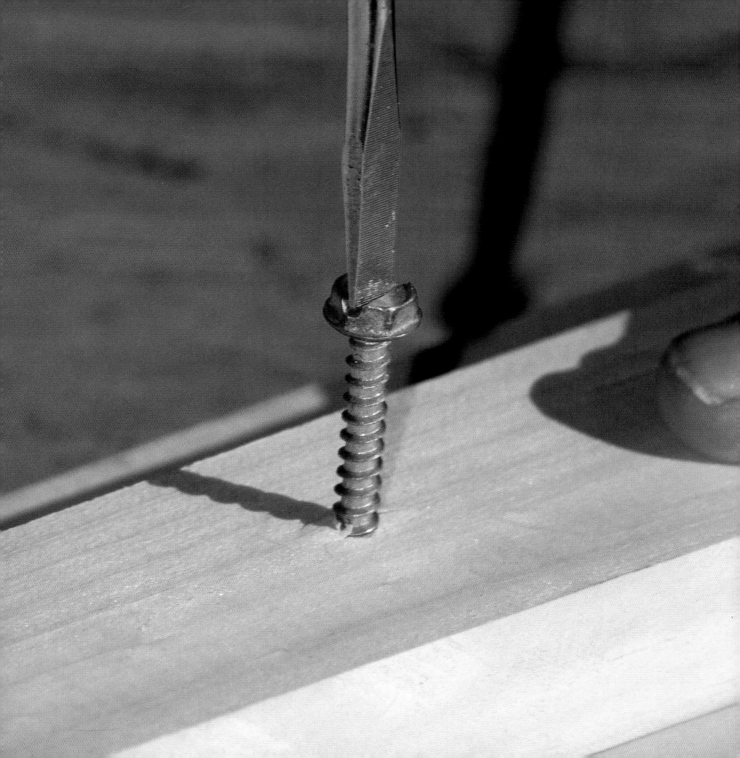

Simple Machines

Simple machines make work easier or faster. Work is using a force to move an object across a distance. Moving, joining things together, and lifting are all kinds of work. A screw is a simple machine that helps people do work.

force
anything that changes the speed, direction, or motion of an object

5

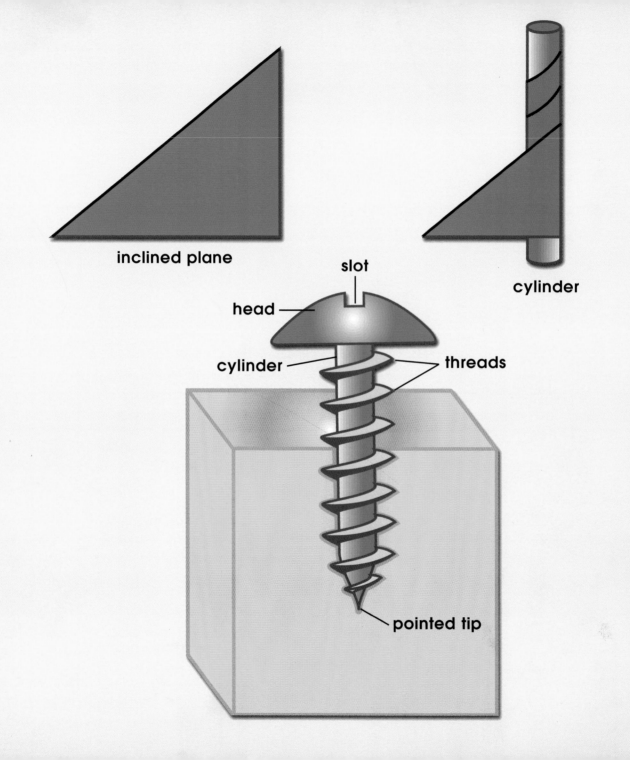

inclined plane

cylinder

slot

head

cylinder

threads

pointed tip

Parts of a Screw

A screw is an inclined plane wound around a cylinder. The inclined plane forms threads. Most screws have a pointed tip. The top of a screw is called a head. The head has a slot for a screwdriver.

cylinder
a tube-shaped object

Using Screws to Join

Screws join two or more objects together. Large screws hold pieces of furniture together. Smaller screws hold parts of toys together. Tiny screws hold eyeglass frames together.

9

Using Screws to Grip

The threads of a screw help grip
objects. A vise has two jaws that
hold objects steady. A screw opens
and closes the jaw. A person turns the
vise handle to tighten the screw. The
threads of the screw allow the vise to
hold objects tightly.

Threads to Threads

A screw's threads can fit into other sets of threads. Threads wind around the opening of a toothpaste tube. Threads inside the cap match the threads on the tube. The two sets of threads grip each other to keep the cap tight.

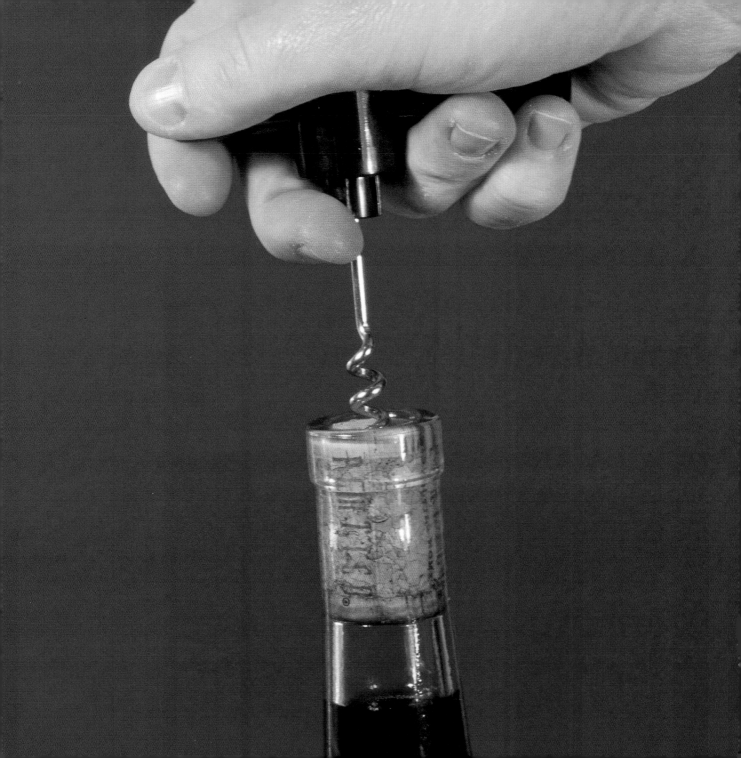

Using Screws to Lift

People use screws to lift objects that are pressed tightly against something. A person cannot lift a cork out of a bottle without a corkscrew. A corkscrew twists into the cork and grips it. A person can then lift the cork out of the bottle.

nut

Tight Hold

Bolts are screws with a flat tip. Bolts have many threads that are close together. A nut holds a bolt in place. A nut also has threads inside it. Workers must turn bolts many times to join parts. Workers use nuts and bolts to hold metal and wooden parts together tightly.

VALLEY PARK ELEMENTARY LIBRARY

Easy to Turn

Threads on some screws wind loosely from one end to the other. A jar and lid have loose threads that fit together. The lid twists off with only a few turns.

Screws in Complex Machines

Simple machines often are part of complex machines. Snowblowers are complex machines. A large screw turns inside a snowblower. The screw helps to break up and push snow.

complex
having many parts

Hands On: Inclined Planes in Screws

A screw is an inclined plane that winds around a cylinder. This activity will show you how inclined planes are parts of screws.

What You Need

One rectangular piece of paper
Scissors
Marker
1/2-inch (1.2-centimeter) thick wood
    dowel, 3 feet (.9 meter) long
Clear tape

What You Do

1. Cut the paper diagonally from one corner to another. You now have two triangles shaped like inclined planes.
2. Turn over one triangle. The diagonal sides of the triangles should both be to the top left.
3. Mark along the diagonal edge of each triangle with the marker.
4. Tape the right edge of one triangle to the dowel and wind it around the dowel. Tape the triangle at the bottom.
5. Repeat step 4 with the second triangle.
6. Compare the "threads" made by the two triangles.

Steep inclined planes make threads that are far apart. Gradual inclined planes make threads that are closer together. A screw with close threads turns easily. You must use more force to turn screws with threads that are far apart.

Words to Know

cylinder (SIL-uhn-dur)—a tube-shaped object

force (FORSS)—anything that changes the speed, direction, or motion of an object

grip (GRIP)—to hold something tightly

inclined plane (in-KLINDE PLANE)—a flat surface that slants; an inclined plane is a simple machine.

join (JOYN)—to fasten two objects together

thread (THRED)—a spiral ridge that winds around a screw

work (WURK)—using a force to move an object across a distance

Read More

Armentrout, Patricia. *The Screw.* Simple Devices. Vero Beach, Fla.: Rourke, 1997.

Hewitt, Sally. *Machines We Use.* It's Science! New York: Children's Press, 1998.

Hodge, Deborah. *Simple Machines.* Starting with Science. Toronto: Kids Can Press, 1998.

Internet Sites

Inventors Toolbox: Simple Machines
http://www.mos.org/sln/Leonardo/InventorsToolbox.html
School Zone, Simple Machines
http://www.science-tech.nmstc.ca/maindex.cfm?idx=1394&language=english&museum=sat&function=link&pidx=1394
Simple Machines
http://www.fi.edu/qa97/spotlight3/spotlight3.html

Index